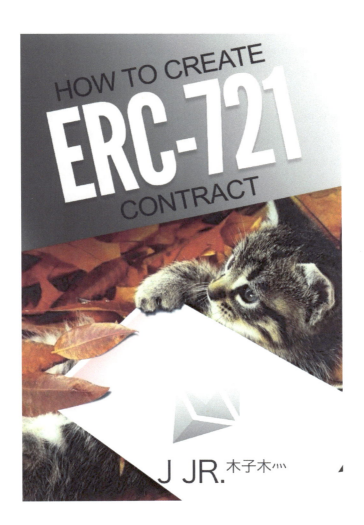

HOW TO CREATE

ERC-721

CONTRACT

J JR.木子木灬

1   Description

Token standard ERC-721 was designed to address the necessities within core developer Ethereum community. The primary purpose is to assist the development of applications for tracking ownership and trading physical assets or digital non-fungible assets. The ERC-721 tokens are different from each other.

The contracts implemented the standards to track a randomly large number of tokens ERC-721 known as non-fungible or NFT tokens or endeavors. A single contract may have 1 or even more of these tokens.

ERC-721 deeds or tokens are titles of ownership for property in the shape of digital assets. Title deeds can increase several opportunities in the digital world. These opportunities are impossible with ERC-20. The tokens can be a license, track and mark ownership of particular assets. These are labeled by assigning the corresponding item of toke in the real world like ID of a token and reading the hash of transaction.

In this draft, you can learn the importance of ERC-721, its standards and the way to create ERC-721 contracts. These contracts can be easy to develop with the help of some simple software. This draft has sample codes and exemplary work for your assistance.

For your convenience, some useful links are available. You can consider these links and sources to create your personalized ERC-721 contracts.

2   Introduction

Since the launch of CryptoKitties app, it is reportedly seen that $12 million value of ether spent in trading and buying different digital unique cats on its particular platform. The decentralized application is famous because it can slow down the average time of the transaction on Ethereum network, sparkle conversation on different online forums about growing pains of the network. It allows developers to tackle different scalability issues. The main focus is on the powerful features of Cryptokitties as ERC-721 token aka NFT (non-fungible token).

3   Defining Fungibility

A set of different assets having equal value is defined as fungible. For instance, a dollar of the United States has the similar value as other dollars of the USA. The person who is spending these dollars and other person receiving these dollars don't care about the movement of these dollars, such as the source of coming and place of landing. The crypto-asset world promotes fungibility as highly liquid assets among other tokens in the ecosystem.

All tokens of blockchain are equally created, and multiple transactions may occur instantaneously and rapidly without annoying participants. All tokens have the similar value so no one will take care of it. The non-fungible assets are not equal to their counterparts. Several tangible examples of these assets are collectibles. Keep it in mind that a baseball has an unusually small value until Babe Ruth sign on it. After the sign, the ball gets extra value and becomes one non-fungible asset. The value of this baseball is different from several other balls.

Non-fungible assets have great scarcity as compare to fungible assets. Hence, these assets hold unique and intrinsic values. Rarity and value are measurable in digital monarchy through distributed ledgers and blockchain. The world is just noticing the potential of digital non-fungible assets.

4   Understand the meaning of ERC

ERC means Ethereum Request for Comments. The community developers of Ethereum author ERC in the shape of the memo describing methods, innovations applicable, research or behaviors to the working of Ethereum ecosystem.

It is acquiesced either for aristocrat review or conveys new information or concepts. After core community and developers approval, the proposals become a particular standard. Therefore, there are set of proposals or standards (e.g., for tokens). In fact, these regulations contain a plain set of tasks via one solo interface. The standards of ERC-20 are the best examples. Smart contracts executing this standard, by evasion may be mentioned to crypto interactions without additional technical work.

5   What is ERC-20?

It is the well-known and common standard within crypto communities. Almost 99% of ICO issued tokes over the top of Ethereum implements the standard. The main benefit is that smart contracts or any other application can interact with the token in a particular standard manner without obtaining details of a token.

Hence, there is a pleasant method to create ICO tokens. A standard method helps you to interact with all tokens as if they are similar. For example, developers of the crypto wallet may avoid integrations and custom development. They must know the address of Ethereum token to implement the particular standards.

```
contract ERC20 {

    function transfer(address _to, uint256 _amount) returns (bool
    success);

    function transferFrom(address _from, address _to, uint256 _amount)
    returns (bool success);

    function balanceOf(address _owner) constant returns (uint256
    balance);

    function approve(address _spender, uint256 _amount) returns (bool
    success);

    function allowance(address _owner, address _spender) constant
    returns (uint256 remaining);

    function totalSupply() constant returns (uint);

}
```

6 What is ERC-721?

The major purpose of this proposal is to create non-fungible tokens. In ERC-223 and ERC-20 standards, you can get a supply of fungible tokens (i.e. solo unit of a token is parallel to another unit).

With its help, you can easily trade these tokens and whole supply of the token can be treated in the similar manner. There are different cases when you may need unidentical tokens that are utilized within a platform, price them in a different manner, and add extra parameters.

For example, you may have tokens that represent some section of real estate entity, and every token have different added parameters. With these standards, the procedure of creating marketplaces can be easy for different types of non-fungible tokens.

```
contract ERC721 {
    // ERC20 compatible functions
    function name() constant returns (string name);
    function symbol() constant returns (string symbol);
    function totalSupply() constant returns (uint256 totalSu
    function balanceOf(address _owner) constant returns (uin
    // Functions that define ownership
    function ownerOf(uint256 _tokenId) constant returns (add
    function approve(address _to, uint256 _tokenId);
    function takeOwnership(uint256 _tokenId);
    function transfer(address _to, uint256 _tokenId);
    function tokenOfOwnerByIndex(address _owner, uint256 _in
    // Token metadata
    function tokenMetadata(uint256 _tokenId) constant return
    // Events
    event Transfer(address indexed _from, address indexed _t
    event Approval(address indexed _owner, address indexed _
}
```

7   ERC-20 vs. ERC-721

Several tokens built off in the blockchain Ethereum are ERC-20 tokens. These tokens are highly liquid and useful and help you to increase billions of dollars via ICOs. Several serve as efficacy tokens that allow token holders to access a specific dApp and its services.

Tokens of ERC-721 are tenaciously non-fungible. The design of ERC-721 tokens given them particular set of invisible and unique properties. These properties are unequal to tokens on the blockchain.

Unlike specific ERC-20 tokens that may be divided almost infinitesimally (a strong tool for the future with crowd-lending or micro-lending distribution). ERC-721 tokens can't be divided because they represent a unique asset in entireness (the similar method the Babe Ruth's sign on the baseball can't be divided in half and manage its value.

Detonation of CryptoKitties demonstrates that ERC-721 tokens may usher in the crypto-collectibles world, where individuals identify unique scarcity on blockchain similar to the practice of physical world.

8   Future of ERC-721 Tokens

Outside the world of crypto-collectibles, though, CryptoKitties becomes an interesting case for the tokenized future, where each physical asset is represented on the NFTs and blockchain. The assets are valuable for their practical utility, collectible and intrinsic value.

You can see the future where houses and land plots or stocks are owned and tracked through blockchain ERC-721 tokens. Applications are designed for Ethereum like Decentraland are building virtual worlds to trade non-fungible assets between users in an ecosystem.

9   Anatomy of ERC-721

Previously, we have mentioned cryptokitties. It is an interesting game positioned around collectible, adorable and breedable creatures known as CrypoKitties. Every cat is fully owned by you and no one can replicate, destroy or taken away this cat.

It is the first game in the world that is built on the advanced blockchain technology. It is the same breakthrough that makes other things practical like Ethereum and Bitcoin. Ether and Bitcoin are cryptocurrencies, but CryptoKitties are actually cryptocollectibles. You are allowed to trade, sell or buy your kitties just like traditional collectibles. This game is special because players can breed, trade, sell and buy digital cats.

Kitty 2641   Kitty 2640

Collectibles are not restricted to digital moggies. Humans have a long history of gathering things. From Pokémon cards to physical coins, people love collecting different things. An important hobby forms interest in different scarce items. Value of commodities is linked to its scarcity and the value of collectible items is connected to their rareness.

You can imitate collectible rare items with Ethereum tokens. Every token follows new standards in ERC-721 Ethereum community. Ethereum appeal for 721 comments or ERC-721 is an important proposal of Ethereum in the end of 2017 by Dieter Shirley. It is a projected standard that may permit tradeable operations of smart contracts like ERC20. Tokens of ERC-721 are unique and non-fungible.

10 Fungible

Something like commodity or money or anything of same nature or quantity can be swapped by another quantity or equal part in the settlement of an account or payment of a debt. Fungibility is an important character of token or asset that determines whether quantities or items of similar type may be complete interchangeable during utility or exchange. For instance, the five dollar bill of the United States can be useful to purchase a can of soda from one convenience store.

The note has value and you can use it for the purchase of an item of more or less worth. Although, when a person goes to buy soda with a baseball card, the owner of a store will not accept it. The reason behind this discrimination is the specific characteristics of $5 and baseball card. A colorful baseball card has some value for children, but not for storeowners. The exclusive attributes of dollar bill and baseball card make them fungible. Their value is different based on the conversation and can't be utilized interchangeably.

For collectible items, two particular items in one collection are not fungible if they contain different characteristics. For different physical coins, a coin made of gold can't be fungible with one copper coin because of their different features and characteristics. They both have ability to give different values to gatherers.

Tokens of ERC-721 are possible to use in an exchange but their values have rareness and uniqueness allied with every token. The standards define the purposes: tokenMetadata, tokeofOwnerByIndenx, transfer, takeownership, approve, ownerof, balanceof, totalsupply, symbol, and name. It defines two important events like Approval and Transfer.

11   Example of ERC-721 Contract

Keep it in mind that the below code is for educational purpose only. The code is not tested so don't implement in your production applications.

11.1   ERC20-similar Functions

ERC-721 describes some functions that offer it some acquiescence with the token standard ERC20. The purpose of this compliance is to make it easy for current wallets to display simple details of the token. These functions allow smart contracts – that fit this standard – act like common cryptocurrencies, such as Ethereum or Bitcoin by describing functions. These functions allow users to perform different actions like sending tokens to other people and verifying the balance of accounts.

11.2   Name

With this function, you can tell the name of token to applications and outside contracts. An important example of implementation of this function is as follows:

```
contract MyNFT {
   function name() constant returns (string name){
      return "My Non-Fungible Token";
   }

}
```

11.3   Symbol

With this function, it is possible to provide compatibility to ERC-721 with the token standard of ERC20. It offers outside programs with shorthand symbol or name of token.

```
contract MyNFT {
   function symbol() constant returns (string symbol){
      return "MNFT";

   }

}
```

11.4   TotalSupply

With this function, you can return the actual sum of coins on a blockchain. The supply can't be constant.

```
contract MyNFT {
  // This can be an arbitrary number

  uint256 private totalSupply = 1000000000;

  function totalSupply() constant returns (uint256 supply){
    return totalSupply;

  }

}
```

11.5   BalanceOf

With this function, you can find some tokens that are owned by a particular address.

```
contract MyNFT {
  mapping(address => uint) private balances;

  function balanceOf(address _owner) constant returns (uint balance)
  {
    return balances[_owner];

  }

}
```

11.6   Ownership Functions

With this function, it is easy to define the way for a contract to handle ownership of token and this ownership is possible to transfer. The notable form of these functions are transfer and takeownership that act similar to send and withdraw functions, respectively. These are important to allow users to transfer tokens among them.

11.7　OwnerOf

You can return the address of an owner for one token with the help of this function. Each ERC-721 token in special for its non-fungible features; hence, unique, it is referenced on blockchain through an exclusive ID. You can easily determine the owner of each token with the help of ID.

```
contract MyNFT {
  mapping(uint256 => address) private tokenOwners;
  mapping(uint256 => bool) private tokenExists;

  function ownerOf(uint256 _tokenId)
  constant returns (address owner) {
    require(tokenExists[_tokenId]);

    return tokenOwners[_tokenId];

  }

}
```

11.8　Approve

With this function, you can grant or approve another entity permission for the transfer of a toke on the behalf of owner. For instance, if 1 MyNFT is owns by Alice, she may call this "approve" function for Bob (her friend). After a prosperous call, friend of Alice could take the ownership of token or perform different operations on these tokens at later time on the behalf of Alice. To see more information on the transfer of ownership, you will need transfer and takeownership functions.

```
contract MyNFT {
  mapping(address => mapping (address => uint256)) allowed;

  function approve(address _to, uint256 _tokenId){
    require(msg.sender == ownerOf(_tokenId));
    require(msg.sender != _to);

    allowed[msg.sender][_to] = _tokenId;
    Approval(msg.sender, _to, _tokenId);

  }

}
```

11.9   TakeOwnership

The function is similar to withdraw function because one outside party may call it to take tokens out of a new account of user. Hence, takeownership may be good to use when users have approved to possess a particular sum of token and wants to withdraw these tokens from the balance of another user.

```
contract MyNFT {
  function takeOwnership(uint256 _tokenId){
    require(tokenExists[_tokenId]);

    address oldOwner = ownerOf(_tokenId);
    address newOwner = msg.sender;

    require(newOwner != oldOwner);

    require(allowed[oldOwner][newOwner] == _tokenId);
    balances[oldOwner] -= 1;
    tokenOwners[_tokenId] = newOwner;

    balances[newOwner] += 1;
    Transfer(oldOwner, newOwner, _tokenId);

  }

}
```

11.10   Transfer

You will need this method to transfer tokens. Transfer allows the owner of each token to send this token to new users, just like standalone cryptocurrencies. Although, a transfer may be initiated in the account receiving has been approved to own a token by sending accounts.

```
contract MyNFT {
  mapping(address => mapping(uint256 => uint256)) private
ownerTokens;
  function removeFromTokenList(address owner, uint256 _tokenId)
private {
    for(uint256 i = 0;ownerTokens[owner][i] != _tokenId;i++){
      ownerTokens[owner][i] = 0;
    }

  }

  function transfer(address _to, uint256 _tokenId){
    address currentOwner = msg.sender;
    address newOwner = _to;

    require(tokenExists[_tokenId]);

    require(currentOwner == ownerOf(_tokenId));
    require(currentOwner != newOwner);
    require(newOwner != address(0));
    removeFromTokenList(_tokenId);

    balances[oldOwner] -= 1;
    tokenOwners[_tokenId] = newOwner;

    balances[newOwner] += 1;
    Transfer(oldOwner, newOwner, _tokenId);

  }

}
```

11.11   tokenofownerByIndex (Recommended – Optional)

Every owner of non-fungible token may own one or even more tokens at a time. Every token may be referenced by an exclusive ID, though, it may be complicated to keep the track of individual tokens own by a user. For this purpose, the contract manages a record of each ID for every owned token. For this reason, each person who has ownership of token may retrieve these tokens by their index in a list of owned tokens. With the help of tokenofownerbyindex, you can retrieve each token.

```
contract MyNFT {
   mapping(address => mapping(uint256 => uint256)) private
ownerTokens;

   function tokenOfOwnerByIndex(address _owner, uint256 _index)
constant returns (uint tokenId){

     return ownerTokens[_owner][_index];

   }

}
```

11.12   Metadata Function

As we have discussed above that non-fungible items are characterized by their specific set of qualities. A colorful baseball card and a dollar can't be fungible because of their different characteristics. Yet, storing data on a blockchain that explain the defining qualities of every token is expensive and it is not recommended. To manage this, you can use store reference, such as HTTP(s) link or IPFS hash, to every attribute of token on a chain so that other programs outside a chain can easily execute logics. This execution allows you to get more information of the token. These references are metadata or data on data.

11.13   tokenMetadata (Recommended – Optional)

With this function, you can discover metadata of a token or the link to this data.

```
contract MyNFT {
  mapping(uint256 => string) tokenLinks;

  function tokenMetadata(uint256 _tokenId) constant returns (string
infoUrl) {
    return tokenLinks[_tokenId];

  }

}
```

11.14   Events

Events can be fired every time a contract gives a call and they are broadcasted to listening programs after they are fired. External programs pay attention to blockchain events so that they may execute logic almost once the occasion is fired with the use of information provided by an event. The standard or ERC-721 defines two important events, such as:

11.15   Transfer

An event is fired every time a token modified hands. It is broadcasted when the ownership of a token is moved from a user to another. It obtains the details of a token's sender that account received a token and that token (via ID) was transferred.

```
contract MyNFT {
  event Transfer(address indexed _from, address indexed _to, uint256
_tokenId);

}
```

11.16   Approval

The event is fired on every occasion when one user approves to transfer ownership of one token to another user. It is possible every time when you execute approval. It details the current ownership of token and account that can get the ownership of this token in the future. It also give details of ID for the transfer of ownership.

```
contract MyNFT {
  event Approval(address indexed _owner, address indexed _approved,
uint256 _tokenId);

}
```

Similar to ERC20, the proposed standard ERC-721 has unlocked a doorway for smart contracts to act as different non-fungible items. You can see them in different applications like CryptoPunks, Decentraland, CryptoKitties and other non-fungible tokens. These tokens have high demand. This standard has potential to expand the economy of cryptocurrency and advance this field to a new level. The ERC-721 is undergoing revisions for advanced developments in the future.

12   Understand the Standards of ERC-721

The ERC-721 norm is a draft standard to create NFT (non-fungible token contracts. Non-fungible term explains that this token is not interchangeable. A dollar (coin) is fungible because if you can exchange a dollar coin for similar coin, without increasing or decreasing its value. Though, if you get a pet cat, and give a pet cat to sender, you may not feel happy because these are not entirely interchangeable. In fact, these are non-fungible.

The Cryptokitties demonstrated the designing of non-fungible assets and allowed players to trade them on Ethereum blockchain. The game requires players to trade and breed kitties, but these kitties are restricted to blockchain. If you don't have access to blockchain, you can't get them. In contrast, customary online games allow you to store data on a main server and admin of the game can make necessary changes. In Cryptokitties, all players can sell and buy their kitties on trustless and decentralized network. Ownership of their kitties are indubitably provable. If you have a kitty, the blockchain is enough to prove that it belongs to you.

You may think that it is only a game with imaginary cats. The main objective of cryptokitties was to prove that it is possible to create and trade non-fungible assets on blockchain. Imagine that the NFT could epitomize the endeavor to a residence instead of cats. You would get a chance to sell these tokens to someone else and get payment and ownership of token without any expenditure of middlemen or expensive lawyers.

Actually, Cryptokitties is a way to introduce the idea of NFT standards to Ethereum communities. This idea converted into a proposal and this proposal converted into a draft for particular standards. These standards are ERC-721 that people have nowadays. The 721 number is not meaningful, it is just 721st improvement proposal of Ethereum on Github.

13   Actual Meaning of ERC Standard

ERC standards represent a particular set of regulations that allows your contract play well with other contracts of developers or software, website or DApp, etc. By offering some important guidelines for desired functions and a few restrictions on their behavior, other programmers may get an ability to write code. The code should have ability to interact with your code without getting access to entire codebase. Here is an example of "balanceof" function defined by this standard:

utility balanceof (address-owner) outside view proceeds (unit 265);

the standard explains that ERC-721 contract should include this important utility. It should take an address (one argument) and should return the actual number of tokens that an address owns (one unit – these non-fungible tokens are impossible to divide)/

This standard has nothing to do with the working pattern of a function. It can be simple, such as returning the mapping value or involves a complicated set of call from internal function and equations. The standard only focuses on one thing that when a person calls "balanceof" on a particular address, they obtain a unit with actual balance of this address.

A standard doesn't care about working pattern of a function because in several cases, there should be extra restrictions or instructions. For balanceof function, this standard has some particular restrictions. See below:

/// @dev NFTs assigned to zero address are invalid, and the function flings for enquiries about a zero address.

So, when a person calls

Balanceof (0x0)

In this situation, the function should throw one error. While writing a complaint for ERC-721 contract, you should adhere all functions to their rules.

Keep it in mind that standards can't prevent you from adding additional rules or function to contract. Your additions should not conflict with laid out rules of a standard. Without any error, additions are perfectly acceptable. Before writing a standard, make sure to particularly follow all rules. It will be good to return to ERC-721 standards while writing your contracts from scratch.

If you can follow the rules of ERC-721, your NFT contracts will become a compliant. Compliance is always necessary because it can make it possible for other folks to get advantage of your token. If a token is easy to use, people can adopt it.

14   Tips to Build Your Own ERC-721 Token

Software like truffle can make your life easy. To start your work, install Truffle:

```
$ npm install -g truffle
```

Now start creating a project with ToboHashToken and the name of this project directory is tobohash.

```
$ mkdir tobohas && cd tobohash
$ truffle (software name) init
$ npm init #verify every default values
```

The complete ERC-721 standard is not small. Here you can see the implementation of the token standard ERC-721 from solidity library zeppelin. For this purpose, you have to include zeppelin-solidity to dependencies.

```
Dollar ($) npm connect zeppelin-solidity –secure-dev
```

After getting zeppelin, you can create a contract.

```
Dollar ($) touch tobohashtoken/contracts.sol
```

To manage compatibility with development of truffle pipeline, you have to create one migration file:

```
Dollar ($) touch relocations/2_use_contracts.js
```

You can follow the given instructions.

```
Var ToboHashToken = relics / artifacts.needed("ToboHashToken");
Module.exports = deployer(function) {
    Deploy.deployer(ToboHashToken);
};
```

It is time to inherit from token ERC-721

```
Pragma firmness ^0.4.21;
ingress 'zeppelin-solidty/contracts/token/ERC-721/ERC-721Token.sol';
contract ToboHashToken ERC-721Token ("ToboHashToken", "THT") {
…
```

Two influences of base class constructor are name of token and symbol of token respectively. Next you have to find out how these tokens are issued. You can make these things as simple as you can. A token can be created in a way that one can add his/her own exclusive instances in the token.

```
Contract ToboHashToken ERC-721Token ("ToboHashToken", "THT") {
    Function produce () public {
        Unit 264 tokenId = alltokens.length + 1;
        _mint(msg.sender, Idoftoken);
    }
```

Notice the code scrap and you will realize that you have to involve its inner –mint function that manages the whole production procedure. Congratulations, the implementation of ERC-721 token is finished now.

Fortunately, this token doesn't require extra work to convert into one naming service. Users of this service can claim their emails, identifiers and names. You must allow users to pass particular identifiers to "create" function and store this function is some type of mapping.

```
contract ToboHashToken is ERC-721Token("ToboHashToken", "THT") {
    mapping(uint264 => cord) inner tokenIdToName;
    mapping(cord => uint264) inner nameToTokenId;
    function generate(cord name) community {
        need(nameToTokenId[name] == 0);
        unit264 tokenId = allTokens.length + 1; and
        _mint(name.msg.sender, tokenId); and
        tokenIdToName[tokenId] = name; and
        nameToTokenId[name] = tokenId;
```

```
    }
and
purpose getTokenName(uint264 tokenId) see community returns (cord){
    return tokenIdToName[tokenId];
}
purpose getTokenId(cord name) see community returns (unit) {
        return nameToTokenId[name];
```

This revers mapping can be helpful for users to check identifier of particular Id of token.

15   Avatar of Token

Tokens are abstracts so it can be satisfying for users if tokens are easy to visualize. Cryptokitties tokens use svg/png images for representation that are served from backend and similar story goes for almost all collectibles. It is possible to remotely represent a token.

Each user have to establish a particular identity that will be implemented as non-fungible tokens.

16   Deploying a Contract for Token

You can use truffle to deploy a contract because you can finish your work by configuring destination of your network. To have access to Ethereum network, Infura can be a good choice. Deploying contracts require some Ether and truffle need access to your wallet. If you want to avoid penetration of your private key in source code, you can use dotenv module.

Start your work by installing all needed modules to deploy Infura.

```
$ (dollar) npm install –secure-dev dotenv wallet-truffle-provider
(currency name) ethereumjs- wallet
```

It is time to modify truffle.js and make the following additions:

```
need('dotenv').config({ trail: '.env.local' }); and
const Webthree = need("web3"); and
const webthree = latest Web3(); and
const ProviderofWallet = need("truffle-ewallet-provider");
const eWallet = need('ethereumjs-wallet');
and
module.exports = {
    internal networks: {
        ropsten: {
            nameofprovider: purpose(){
                var ropstenPersonalKey = latest
Buffer(process.env["ROPSTEN_PERSONAL_KEY"], "hex")
                var ropsteneWallet =
eWallet.fromPersonalKey(ropstenPersonalKey);
                return latest WalletProvider(ropstenWallet,
"https://ropsten.infura.io/");
            },
            gas: 4600000,
            gasCost: web3.toWei("twenty", "gwei"),
            network_id: 'three',
        }
    }
};
```

Now you will open .env.local and carefully paste in personal key, such as:

```
ROPSTEN_PERSONAL_KEY= "123writeryourpersonalkeyhere"
```

It is important to add .env.local to gitignore.

Several test networks of ethereum are available to test your cotnracts like Rinkeyby or Kovan. We have used Rosten ETH in this tutorial because it is convenient for every user. All networks are almost similar and you are free to use testnet.

You can visit faucet.metamash.io for test ETH. After getting a few ETH from faucet, you are ready to deploy them. Once you have everything to deploy, just execute:

```
$ truffle deploy (install) -network ropsten
```

You have to copy the appropriate address from output into Etherscan Ropsten search box and paste it. You can see a newly installed contract.

To claim one token, go to remix.ethereum.org and remove all current code. You have to paste in the given snippet.

```
pragma firmness ^0.4.21;
contract ToboHashToken {
    purpose generate(cord name) community;
}
```

If you have one contract interface, you have to call its procedure. After doing this, you can switch to a "Run" tab located on the right side of Remix screen. Paste address of contact in an appropriate field and hit "at address". This will generate a creation method that take a parameter. By calling it, everything will be successfully passed. You will become the owner of a unique token ERC-721.

17   Build one Social Layer

Instead of creating an entire site from scratch, you can use a current website because free sample are available online. For instance, userfeeds.github.io/cryptopurr. Here you will learn possible changes required for the support of tobohashtokens.

In the first step, clone cryptopurr to one new directory:

```
$ git replica git@github.com:feedsofuser/cryptopurr.git   and
$ cd cryptopurr    and
$ git reset --hard 0626acd6bb7ce87bcd72cca4d8f1049241e8c0e6
```

You will particularly need the following files:

- **.env:** File with important atmosphere variables to let the app work.
- **package.json**: Standard package.json produce-react-app file with possible scripts and dependencies.
- **src/entityApi.js**: It defines the details of particular token that is drawn from a network and exhibited on sites.
- **public/index.html**: you have to set an appropriate title for an html page
- **Ad One. .env**

You have to set the below properties:

RESPOND_APP_NAME—name of your app (in this case ToboHash).
RESPOND_APP_INTERFACE_WORTH—URL to host your website.

RESPOND_APP_ERC_721_NET— mention the name of network where ERC-721 contract will be deployed. You should notice that your contract will be deployed on special network users and enable them to generate messages on different networks (power of cross-chain).
RESPOND_APP_ ADDRESS_ERC_721 — mention address of ERC-721 contract.
RESPOND_APP_BASENAME—Foundation url (like tobohash-book/)

- **Ad Two. package.json**

Change home_page and name and inset similar values here just like previous file.

- **Ad Three. src/entityApi.js**

You have to change getEntityData purpose. This purpose fetches details of a specific entity from backend. It grosses tokenId as an important parameter and returns one custom object that is utilized to display your entity on a page. If you are working without your backend, you can connect it to your contract on ethereum network. If you are using Infura, it can manage this work for you.

In this task, we are using web3js to connect to Infura. To invoke procedures on contract, you will need ABI (App Binary Interface). You can get it from the tobohash-token plan by appealing the following guidelines:

```
$ (Dollar) truffle compile \
    && kitty build/contracts/ToboHashToken.json | jq '.abi' | xclip
```

Now, paste this into project of tobohash-book:

```
$ mkdirectory src/abi && xyclip -o src/abi/ToboHashToken.json
```

After getting ABI contract, you will be able to use it with address of contract to create an example of representation of javascript contract.

```
import of WebThree from 'web3';
const toboHashTokenArtifacts = need('./abi/ToboHashToken.json');
and
const webthree = new Web3(novel
Web3.providers.HttpServiceProvider('https://ropsten.infura.io/'));
and
const contractExample = new
web3.eth.Contract(toboHashTokenArtifacts.abi,
'0xfa9d471300b0a4cc40ad4dfa5846864973520f45');
This point allows you to call the method of contract so implement the
function of getEntity Data.
You are recommended to appeal getnameoftoken with Identity to get the
name of toke and use getUrloftoke to get tobohash images of your
token.
and
export const obtainEntityData = async entityId => {
    and
    try {
        const TokenNameresponse = wait
contractInstance.procedures.getNameofToken(entityId).call();
        and
        const Nameoftoken = TokenNameresponse.valueOf();
        and
        const TokenUrlresponse= expect
contractInstance.methods.getTokenUrl(tokenName).call();
```

```
        const tokenUrl = responseTokenUrl.valueOf();
        and
        return {
            id: Identity,
            name: Nameoftoken,
            photo_url: tokenUrl, // photo of your entity
            url: `https://tobohash.org`, // site with information of
particular identity
            color: '#444444' // color of background
        };
    } catch (e) {
        console.mistake(e);
        return indeterminate;
    }
};
```

Now you can get Translationsentity that defines displayed texts across an application. You may alter them for suitability of local language and theme of website. You can define these things as follows:

```
export const Translationsentity = {
    Placeholdercomment: '#Hash your tale',
    answerPlaceholder: '#Hash your reply',
    noErrorEntities: 'No tobohashes found',
    NameofEntity: 'ToboHash'
};
```

Map of colors from 4 line defines that suitable color for background behind a kitty. You can have a background hue across a site, you may remove it entirely.

Finally, you have to modify avatarSizes. The top approach for this job is to open an application, find accurate values with the use of console web browser and write them in a file. Once you are ready for everything, your app is here to launch.

To initiate an application:

```
$ (dollar) yarn
$ (dollar) yarn initiate
```

The example of accurate values for avatarSizes were below:

```
export const Sizesofavatar = {
    verySmall: { Sizeofcontainer: '32px', sizeofimage: '32px',
OffsetimgTop: '50%', LeftimgOffset: '50%' },
    small: { Sizeofcontainer: '44px', sizeofimage: '44px',
OffsetimgTop: '50%', LeftimgOffset: '50%' },
    medium: { Sizeofcontainer: '54px', sizeofimage: '54px',
OffsetimgTop: '50%', LeftimgOffset: '50%' },
    large: { Sizeofcontainer: '64px', sizeofimage: '64px',
OffsetimgTop: '50%', LeftimgOffset: '50%' }
};
```

- **Ad four. public/index.html**

23 line allows you to modify the title.

Now you are finished with your social platform for collectibles. The application contains of frontend (the ethereum network takes care of backend). You may deploy it with the use of github pages.

Finally, if you want to duplicate this coding for yourself, you can get codes in the below repositories:

https://github.com/Userfeeds/robohash-token

https://github.com/Userfeeds/robohash-book

18 ERC-721 Non-Fungible Standards of Token

These standards allow the implementation of API standards for NFTs in smart contracts. This standard is famous for its great functionality to transfer and track NFTs.

You can consider use cases of NFTs transacted and owned by different individuals and consignments of third party auctioneers, wallets and brokers. NFTs may represent possession over physical or digital assets. You can consider diverse universe assets and know its potential.

- Navigate value of assets: burdens, loans and other liabilities
- Virtual collectables: unique images of collectable cards and kittens
- Physical property: unique artwork and houses

Generally, all houses have distinction because kitties are different. Two kitties can't be similar. NFTs are easy to distinguish and you should track the ownership of every separate kitty.

A standard boundary allows action, broker and wallet applications to work with NFT on Ethereum. You can obtain simple smart ERC-721 contracts to track an arbitrarily large NFTs. See below for additional apps:

The standard of ERC-721 is inspired by ERC-20 token standard. It builds on an experience of two years because after the creation of EIP 20. EIP-20 is not sufficient to track NFTs because every asset in non-fungible distinct whereas every quantity of token is undistinguishable (fungible).

Alteration between EIP-20 and this standard is explained below:

Specifications:

The keywords "OPTIONAL, MAY, RECOMMENDED, SHOULD NOT, SHOULD, SHALL NOT, SHALL, REQUIRED, MUST NOT and MUST in the document to interpret as mentioned in 2119 RFC."

Each ERC-721 compliance contract should implement ERC165 and ERC-721 interfaces (subject to cautions below):

```solidity
pragma solidity ^0.4.20;

/// @title Non-Fungible ERC-721 Token Standard
/// @dev See https://github.com/ethereum/EIPs/blob/master/EIPS/eip-
721.md
///  Note: the identifier ERC-165 for this particular interface is
0x80ac58cd.
interface ERC-721 /* is ERC165 */ {
    /// @dev releases NFT differences by any instrument.
    ///  The event releases the creation of NFTs (`from` == 0) and
destroyed
    ///  (`to` == 0).  Exception: creation of contract during NFTs
    ///  it is possible to create or assign without a transfer
discharge, at the current moment of
    ///  any transmission, the permissible address for the NFT (if
available) is reorganize to none.
    Transfer event (address is indexed _from, and address indexed _to
uint264 indexed _tokenId);
```

```solidity
    /// @dev it emits with the change in approved NFT address
    ///   reaffirmed.  The zero address indicates there is no approved
address.
    ///   When a Transfer occasion emits, it can be an indication for
approval
    ///   address for that NFT (if any) is reset to none.
    event Authorization(address indexed _owner, dissertation indexed
_approved, uint264 indexed _tokenId);

    /// @dev it emits when one operator is permitted or incapacitated
for a proprietor.
    ///   The functioning can achieve all NFTs for a proprietor.
    event endorsementforall (address indexed _owner, address indexed
_operative, bool _permitted);

    /// @notification Count complete set of NFTs allocated to a
proprietor
    /// @dev NFTs allocated to one zero address and these are
considered inacceptable, and the
    ///   function heaves for enquiries about the zero address.
    /// @param _proprietor a declaration for whom to request the
equilibrium
    /// @return actual quantity of NFTs possessed by `_possessor`,
possibly zero
    purpose balanceOf (owner_address) outside sight returns (uint264)

    /// @notice search the possessor of one NFT
```

```
    /// @dev assigned NFTs to zero address is invalid, and requests
    ///  about these addresses do toss.
    /// @param _Idoftoken an identifier for one NFT
    /// @return an address of an owner of one NFT
    purpose ownerOf(uint264 _Idoftoken) exterior sight returns
(address);

    /// @notice Relocation of the possession of one NFT from an
address to a new address address
    /// @dev throws unless `msg.sender` is the present possessor, an
official
    ///  operator, or allowable address for a NFT.  Pitches if
`_from` is
    ///  not the present owner.  Throws if `_to` is a zero address.
Throws if
    ///  `_tokenId` isn't a lawful NFT.  When transmission is
complete, this function
    ///  checks if `_to` is one smart contract (code size > 0).  If
so, it calls
    ///  `onERC-721Received` on `_to` and throws if the return value
is not
    ///  `bytes4(keccak256("onERC-
721Received(address,address,uint256,bytes)"))`.
    /// @param _from a present owner of the NFT
    /// @param _to a new owner
    /// @param _tokenId The NFT to transfer
```

```
/// @param data Additional data with no specified format, sent in
call to `_to`
    function safeTransferFrom(address _from, address _to, uint256
_tokenId, bytes data) external payable;


    /// @notice Transfers the ownership of an NFT from one address to
another address
    /// @dev it works identically to the other function with an extra
data parameter,
    ///   except this function just sets data to "".
    /// @param _from a present owner of the NFT
    /// @param _to a new owner
    /// @param _tokenId The NFT to transfer
    function safeTransferFrom(address _from, address _to, uint256
_tokenId) external payable;


    /// @notice Transfer ownership of an NFT -- THE CALLER IS
RESPONSIBLE
    ///   TO AUTHORIZE THAT `_to` IS ACCOMPLISHED OF GETTING NFTS OR
ELSE
    ///   THEY CAN BE ETERNALLY LOST
    /// @dev throws unless `msg.sender` is the present owner, an
authorized
    ///   operator, or the approved address for this NFT.  Throws if
`_from` is
    ///   not the current owner.  Throws if `_to` is the zero address.
Throws if
```

```
    ///  `_tokenId` is not a valid NFT.
    /// @param _from The current owner of the NFT
    /// @param _to The new owner
    /// @param _tokenId The NFT to transfer
    function transferFrom(address _from, address _to, uint256
_tokenId) external payable;


    /// @notice Change or reaffirm the approved address for an NFT
    /// @dev The zero address indicates there is no approved address.
    ///  Throws unless `msg.sender` is the current NFT owner, or an
authorized
    ///  operator of the current owner.
    /// @param _approved The new approved NFT controller
    /// @param _tokenId The NFT to approve
    function approve(address _approved, uint256 _tokenId) external
payable;


    /// @notice Enable or disable approval for a third party
("operator") to manage
    ///  all of `msg.sender`'s assets
    /// @dev Emits the ApprovalForAll event.  The contract MUST allow
    ///  multiple operators per owner.
    /// @param _operator Address to add to the set of authorized
operators
    /// @param _approved True if the operator is approved, false to
revoke approval
```

```solidity
    function setApprovalForAll(address _operator, bool _approved)
external;

    /// @notice Get the approved address for a single NFT
    /// @dev Throws if `_tokenId` is not a valid NFT.
    /// @param _tokenId The NFT to find the approved address for
    /// @return The approved address for this NFT, or the zero
address if there is none
    function getApproved(uint256 _tokenId) external view returns
(address);

    /// @notice Query if an address is an authorized operator for
another address
    /// @param _owner The address that owns the NFTs
    /// @param _operator The address that acts on behalf of the owner
    /// @return True if `_operator` is an approved operator for
`_owner`, false otherwise
    function isApprovedForAll(address _owner, address _operator)
external view returns (bool);
}

interface ERC165 {
    /// @notice Query if a contract implements an interface
    /// @param interfaceID The interface identifier, as specified in
ERC-165
    /// @dev Interface identification is specified in ERC-165.  This
function
```

```solidity
    ///  uses less than 30,000 gas.
    /// @return `true` if the contract implements `interfaceID` and
    ///  `interfaceID` is not 0xffffffff, `false` otherwise
    function supportsInterface(bytes4 interfaceID) external view
returns (bool);
}
```

19   Understand the Meaning of Important Terms in Coding

If you are taking interest in Ethereum, it is essential to learn the terminologies and their definitions. Here are a few frequently used terms and their definitions.

19.1   Ð (Stands for ETH)

D with a stroke is a word used in Icelandic, Middle English, Faroese and Old English. It stands for "ETH". It is frequently used in words like Ðapp (decentralized application) or ÐEV. In these words, Ð represents Norse letter "eth". The uppercase Ð "ETH" symbolizes the Dogecoin (cryptocurrency).

19.2   Dapp (Decentralized Application)

It is a service operated without a main trusted party. This application enables direct communication, agreements and interaction between resources and end users without any middleman.

19.3   DAO

DAO is decentralized autonomous organization. It is a particular type of contract on blockchain that is enforced, automate or codify the working of a company, including expansion, spending, operations, fund-raising, and governance.

19.4   Identity

A set of cryptographically demonstrable interactions has property created by a similar person.

19.5　　Digital Identity

The particular set of cryptographically certifiable transactions signed by similar communal key describe the behavior of digital identity. In numerous scenarios of the real world, it is necessary that arithmetical identities overlap with identities of the real world. Confirming this without any violence is a mysterious problem.

19.6　　Unique Identity

The particular set of cryptographically certifiable interactions has property that was created by a similar person with added constraints that a person can't have numerous unique identities.

19.7　　Reputation

Property of a character that other objects believe that character can be either (a) competent at a particular task, or (b) trustworthy to a context, i.e. not to deceive others, even for a short-term profit.

19.8　　Escrow

If two entities (mutually-untrusting) are involved in business, they may desire to pass funds through a 3rd party (mutually trusted party) and instruct this party to send funds to payees after showing the product delivery evidence. It is essential to decrease the risk of payee or payer committing fraud. Both the 3rd party and construction party is known as escrow.

19.9　　Deposit

It is a digital property put into a particular contract involving a second party like if particular conditions are unsatisfied, this property will be automatically surrendered and credited to the counterparty as an insurance against conditions, or donated to a charitable fund or destroyed.

19.10   Web of Trust

If X highly rated Y and Y highly rated Z, then X is trusting Z. Powerful and complicated mechanism to determine the reliability of a particular individual in particular concepts may theoretically be collected from this standard.

19.11   Incentive Compatibility

Incentive-compatibility is a protocol if everyone is following the rules and doing well than trying to cheat, at least lots of people are agreed to cheat together at the similar time.

19.12   Collusion

In the scenario of an incentivized protocol, when numerous participants conspire (play) together to game the particular rules to their benefits.

19.13   Token System

It involves tradeable fungible virtual good. More officially, a token structure is a databank mapping addresses to figures with property that the key permitted operation is a transfer of N tokens from X – Y, with particular conditions that N is non-negative, N is lesser than current balance of X and a document approving the transfer is numerically signed by X. secondary "consumption" and "issuance" operations can exist and transaction fees are collected and instantaneous multi-transfers with numerous parties can be possible. Usual use cases are digital gift cards, company shares, cryptographic tokes in networks, and currencies.

19.14   Block

A data package has zero or even more transactions, the hash of parent block (previous) and other data. The total blocks, with each block except for the early "genesis block" encompassing the hash of its previous blocks known as blockchain and have the whole transaction history of the network.

Keep it in mind that some cryptocurrencies (blockchain-based) use a word "ledger" as a substitute of blockchain and these two words are approximately equivalent, though in systems that utilize the ledger term, every block contains a copy of present state (for instance, registrations, partially completed contracts and currency balances) of each account allowing its users to dispose of obsolete historical data.

19.15   Dapp

Đapp means decentralized application. It is pronounced as Ethapp because of the utilization of uppercase ETH letter Đ.

19.16   Address

An address of Ethereum represents one account. For EOA, it is derived as last 20 bytes of the communal key controlling an account, such as cd2a3d9f938e13cd947ec05abc7fe734df8dd826.

The hexadecimal format is based on 16 notation. It is indicated openly by affixing 0x to an address. Console function and web3.js accept addresses without or with this prefix, but their use is encouraged for transparency. Since 2 hex characters represent every byte of address and a preceded address contain 42 characters. Several APIs and apps are meant to implement new address scheme (checksum-enabled) in Ethereum Mist wallet as of 0.5.0.

19.17   Hexadecimal

It is a common representation layout for byte sequencing. It is beneficial because the values are epitomized in a particularly compact layout with the use of two characters in each byte (the characters are [0-9] [a-f]).

19.18   Ether

It is the name of Ethereum (a currency). This short name is used for computation within EVM. Obscurely, ether is a unit in this system.

19.19   EOA (Externally Owned Account)

It is an account controlled by one private key. If you have a private key linked with EOA, you can get the ability to send messages and ether from it. All contract accounts have a particular address. Contract accounts and EOAs may combine in a single type of account during Serenity.

19.20   Gas

It is the name of cryptofuel consumed while execitomh codes via EVM. The gas is a payment of performance fee for operation on Ethereum blockchain.

19.21   Gas Limit

The gas limit is useable for individual transactions and blocks (block-gas-limit). For each transaction, the gas boundary signifies the determined gas amount that you want to pay for the execution of the transaction. It is designed for the protection of users from getting exhausted while executing malicious or buggy contracts. The floor of gas limit increases with the introduction of the homestead from 3,141,592 gas – 4,712,388 gas (it is 50% increase).

19.22　Gas Price

The cost in the ether of a gas unit is specified in a transaction. After launching homestead, the default price of gas decrease from 50 Shannon – 20 Shannon (it is 60% decrease).

19.23　Web3

A Web3 paradigm is an important form that refers to a particular occurrence of improved connectedness between decentralization of applications, services, and all types of devices, semantic storage for online information and artificial intelligence apps for the web.

19.24　Epoch

It is an interval between every renewal of DAG utilized as seed by PoW algorithm Ethash. The epoch is defined as 30,000 blocks.

19.25　Cryptography (elliptic curve)

It refers to a particular approach to public-key cryptography on an algebraic arrangement of elliptic arcs over finite fields.

19.26　Wallet

In a generic sense, a wallet is anything that allows you to store ether or other tokens of crypto. In a crypto space, the wallet can be anything from an individual public/private key pair, such as single paper wallet to manage numerous key pairs like Ethereum Mist Wallet.

19.27　Contract

A piece of code on Ethereum blockchain to encompass executable functions and a data set. These functions implement with each Ethereum transaction for particular parameters.

The input parameters decide the execution of functions and interaction with data within and other than a contract.

19.28 Mining

It is a process to verify contract execution and transaction on Ethereum blockchain in an altercation for an incentive in the ether with the help of mining of each block.

19.29 Mining Pool

Pooling of available resources by miners, who share processing power on a network and split reward equally, as per the amount of contribution to solving each block.

19.30 Mining Reward

The total amount of ether (cryptographic tokens) that is offered to the miner who mined a novel block.

19.31 Tate

It refers to a snapshot of data and balances at a specific point in time on the blockchain. It refers to the condition of a specific block.

19.32 Blockchain

It is an ever-growing series of blocks of data that grows with each new transaction. Every new block becomes the part of blockchain and chained to current blockchain through a cryptographic proof of work.

20 Non-Fungibles Revolt of 2018

Exmples of non-fungible Cryptoc collectibles are Cryptokitties, Pepe Rare Cards and Cryptopunks. At its peak, the ERC-721 contracts account for almost 20 percent of Ethereum traffic and slowing down this network. Equivalent to 10 million of USD are spent on collectibles of crypto at an increasing rate. Several transactions are occurring in the past months. These are resulting in particular media coverage. See some ideas and insights compiled from past experience with building dApps and smart contracts around a particular concept of tokens with non-fungible. Qualities.

21 Influence of ERC20 on ERC-721

The ERC-721 have collaboration with ERC-721 non-fungible standard assets. The standard is heavily based on the tokens of ERC-20. It was written in current implementations and possible common language.

The non-fungible and fungible tokens are different in their interfaces and interactions of users with them to trade and interact them. The resemblance between ERC20 and ERC-721 is a bad thing. In fact, the standard of ERC-721 inherit some problems from ERC20 that is not fixed.

Here are some issues for implementation and testing of various interfaces that interrelate with tokens of ERC-721:

Approve: This function was intended to allow a smart contract to get control over tokens as per particular conditions, notably EtherDelta and ox protocol. Calling favor for each solo asset that you authorize is exceedingly inefficient.

The transferForm and takeOwnership functions seem redundant. Offering the objective of approve is to provide one smart contract to manage your asset, but it is used to transfer this asset to a new address; transferFrom and takeOwnership are syntax flavor, a risky thing for smart contracts. A modest transfer to a contract address is sufficient.

transferFrom (from to assetID) has impractical parameters. From may always infer because from ownerofassetId.

Deficiency of Standardization: It is an important component to standardize images to list the tokens under one category.

Meagre extensibility: you can image that maximum cryptoassets may require you to define a list of features unique to domain like the cyrptokitties (breeding frequency) or Decentraland (land contents). A new standard NFT must permit important improvements and modifications for different cases.

You can see several requires and proposals for an improve standards for fungible tokens. Several plain ERC-20 contracts don't have any method for recovery of tokens. It may lead to loss of over 3,000,000 USD value of tokens, with only 1,000,000 USD in smart EOS contract. Keep it in mind that you have to be careful while drafting one new standard for token.

.

22   Conclusion

ERC-721 defines non-fungible tokens. These are also known as NFT that means non-fungible token. You may find it confusing to understand term non-fungible. The meaning is that each token is not equal to other token. It is completely opposite to ERC20 where tokens are similar to each other.

CryptoKitties is the famous example of ERC-721, where every kitten is known as a token. It is described by a compliant ERC-721 contract with some extra functions. Unlike ERC20, you can't just store tokens in one wallet. Each token has its unique value so you are required to store owner of every token.

NFT allows you to understand several things, such as:

- Number of total tokens
- Number of tokens in particular wallet
- Owner of particular tokens
- Specifications of tokens in particular wallet

Moreover, you can do some actions, such as:

- Transfer ERC-721 tokens to a particular wallet
- Appeal tokens from a particular wallet
- Accept an appeal from a particular wallet

23   Acknowledgement

- Dr. Kung Chen
- Dr. Chang-Wu Chen

- Jo-Yu Duh
- Chen He Lai